BRISTOL FILTON AIRPORT

End of an Era

Leo Marriott

B¹
11/13

Air
Sea
Media

First published in 2013 by Air Sea Media Services, an imprint of
Forty Editorial Services Ltd
www.airseamedia.co.uk

Printed and bound in China

All the photos in this book were taken by the author with the
exception of the monchrome images which come from the
US National Archives via Air Sea Media Services and also a few
colour images supplied by Peter March which are appropriately
credited.

Front Cover: *One of the last Airbus Beluga flights to land
at Filton is appropriately silhouetted against the evening sky.*

Back Cover: *A British Midland Regional Embraer 145
makes the last commercial jet departure from Filton, 21
December 2012.*

CONTENTS

INTRODUCTION

Situated on the northern outskirts of the City of Bristol, Filton Airport could legitimately lay claim to being the oldest continuously operating civil airfield in Britain when it closed at the end of 2012 after no fewer than 102 years of flying operations. This volume is a personal anthology of the last few years of this historic site.

Flying operations, and the construction of aeroplanes, started at Filton around 1910 when the original Bristol Aeroplane Company Ltd. and its associate companies were formed by Sir George White. Many early aviators learnt to fly on Bristol Boxkites and during the First World War the Bristol F.2A/B Fighter was one the most successful British aircraft of the period. Between the wars the company developed a range of aircraft leading up to the Bristol Blenheim light bomber, which first flew in 1936. At that time it was faster

than contemporary fighters, although by the outbreak of war in 1939 this no longer was the case.

A feature of Bristol aircraft was that almost without exception they were powered by Bristol-designed and built aero engines. Indeed, in 1939 the Bristol aircraft and aero engine manufacturing complex at Filton was the largest of its type in the world. During World War II production efforts centred on the Blenheim bomber, the Beaufort torpedo bomber and the Beaufighter multi-role fighter. Naturally Filton presented an obvious target for the Luftwaffe and it was raided many times, the rows of still-extant air raid shelters standing testament to those perilous times.

After 1945 great effort were expended on the design and construction of the Brabazon airliner, at the time and until the advent of the Boeing 747 in 1969, the

Filton is regarded by many as the spiritual home of the Concorde supersonic airliner. The British prototype took off from here in 1969 and the last one returned here in 2003. It is currently destined to be the centrepiece of a projected aviation heritage site.

largest airliner ever built. To accommodate this pioneering aircraft, Filton's runway was widened and extended, necessitating the destruction of the village of Charlton Hayes. Ironically this village name is being resurrected by a new housing development built on land previously forming part of the airport. Unfortunately the Brabazon project was abandoned in 1953 and the succeeding turboprop Britannia, smaller and more conventional, suffered from an overlong gestation period so that by the time it was ready for service the airlines were looking for the new swept-wing jets such as the Boeing 707 and Douglas DC-8.

Often forgotten today is the fact that the Bristol Aeroplane Company was a pioneer in the development of helicopters, but their designs were taken over by Westland Aircraft Ltd. at the instigation of the government and several promising projects were abandoned.

In December 1963 the Bristol Aeroplane Company finally lost its separate identity and became merely a division of the British Aircraft Corporation (BAC) which also absorbed famous names such as Vickers, English Electric and Hunting Aircraft. As such it played a major part in the development of the Concorde supersonic airliner of which the first British prototype (002) flew for the first time at Filton on 9 April 1969, powered by Bristol Siddeley Olympus jet engines. Concorde production ended in 1979 by which time the engine division had been taken over by Rolls-Royce and after that date Filton ceased to be a centre for the manufacture of complete airframes. However as part of BAC and its successor, British Aerospace (BAe), it continued to build major components for aircraft assembled elsewhere such as the complete tail unit for successful BAC-111 twin jet airliner.

In the 1980s and 1990s Filton was the centre for many test-flying programmes, while the aircraft works gained various contracts including one for the maintenance of United States Air Force F-111 bombers based in the UK and the conversion of Airbus A300/310 airliners to freighter configuration. The European Airbus partnership also included BAe who were responsible for wing design and Filton became a centre of expertise for the production of wing and undercarriage components as well as wind tunnel testing. However BAE Systems, the rebranded BAe, decided to sell its share in Airbus in 2008 and from that time the writing was on the wall for the airport at Filton. Although production of components for the Airbus A380 and the new A350XWB, as well as complete wing sets for the A400M freighter, will continue for the foreseeable future, BAE Systems decided that operation of the airport was no longer commercially viable and set a closing date of 21 December 2012 – truly the end of a magnificent era of British pioneering engineering and design.

Below: "And it's goodbye from us!" With the last aircraft departed and the tower shut down, the ATC team marks the end of the line in traditional style. The Author is at front left.

1. FILTON AIRFIELD - A BRIEF HISTORY

Aviation activities at the Filton site began in 1910 when the industrial entrepreneur Sir George White set up the British and Colonial Aeroplane Company Ltd. to build French-designed Zodiac biplanes under a licensing agreement. Factory space was provided by leasing part of the Bristol Tramway Company's depot and repair shop at Filton. The Zodiac proved to be a failure and instead the company began producing a design based on contemporary Farman biplanes, which became the known as the Boxkite. Initially these were sent by road to Larkhill where they were assembled and flown at the flying school set up by the company, but on 14 November 1910 a Boxkite made some demonstration flights from Durdham Down to carry passengers over the Clifton suspension bridge. However, it was not until the following April that the first recorded aircraft movement at Filton occurred when one of the company's pilots, Maurice Tabateau, flew in from Larkhill, although he had to make a forced landing while en route. Subsequently flying operations became more frequent at Filton, using a landing ground within the present manufacturing site although the majority of the company's flight operations still took place at Larkhill and also at Brooklands.

In the years leading up to the outbreak of war in 1914, British and Colonial designed and produced several innovative aircraft including advanced monoplanes and a seaplane equipped with hydrofoils. By 1914 the Bristol Scout biplane was in production and was used by both the Royal Flying Corps (RFC) and the Royal Naval Air Service (RNAS). However, the coming of war had a major impact on the company: its flying schools at Larkhill and

Brooklands were taken over by the War Office while the factory was ordered to prioritise on the production of the B.E.2c two-seater scouts which had been designed by Geoffrey de Havilland at the Royal Aircraft Factory Farnborough. Bristol and Colonial's chief designer, Frank Barnwell, worked on a new two-seater scout which incorporated the

Above: A Bristol F.2A at Filton in 1918. Most production aircraft were powered by a Rolls-Royce Falcon engine with a distinctive circular radiator but the example shown here is one of a few fitted with an RAF.4d air-cooled engine for test purposes. In the background are some of the original aircraft sheds erected at Filton in 1915 and still in existence today.

The Bristol Ten-seater was an early attempt to enter the civil air transport market but met with little success. The prototype, shown here in 1924, was converted as an Express Freight Carrier and was used by Imperial Airways until 1926.

experience gained in the early war years and the result was the F.2A – more universally known as the Bristol Fighter. This first flew on 9 September 1916 and was an instant success. Ordered into full production it rapidly became the RFC's standard fighter-reconnaissance aircraft. A total of 5,308 were delivered, of which 3,921 were built at Filton before production finally ceased in 1927

The onset of war in 1914 and the massive boost in aircraft orders inevitably led to an expansion of the manufacturing site at Filton, which encroached on the previously used landing ground. A new flying ground was, therefore, established

north of the factory towards the end of 1915 and this was the genesis of the airfield as we know it today. To accommodate aircraft and military personnel various buildings were erected on the north side of the airfield bordered by Hayes Lane. These included several timber-framed aircraft sheds clad in corrugated iron – and despite the temporary nature of these structures, two still remain today almost in their original form. As aircraft production from Filton and other centres rose almost exponentially over the years, three larger hangars were erected during 1917 on the north-east side of the airfield alongside the Gloucester Road (A38). These were a standard World War I design with a wooden-framed Belfast truss structure to support the curved roof and all were

Left: The first aircraft to feature the Jupiter radial engine was the Bristol Badger, which first flew in 1919 and was intended as a replacement for the Bristol Fighter although no production orders were forthcoming. The aircraft is parked outside one of the north-east Belfast hangars with the current 501 Hangar just visible in the background.

triple-span hangars. These hangars were allocated to No. 5 Aircraft Acceptance Park (AAP), which took aircraft from Parnall Aircraft at Yate and Westland Aircraft at Yeovil as well as from Filton itself. The APP was then responsible for preparing the aircraft for service before they were issued to operational units. Two more hangars, one triple span and one single, were erected at the Hayes Lane site which was used by the RFC. Subsequently it became an RAF station in 1918 when that service was formed from the amalgamation of the RFC and RNAS.

The coming of peace in November 1918 inevitably resulted in a major contraction of activity at Filton as wartime production contracts were cancelled and the AAP was closed down. For financial and legal reasons, the Bristol and Colonial Aeroplane Company was wound up and its assets transferred to the Bristol Aeroplane Company, which the far-sighted Sir George White had set up as a nominal company as far back as 1910. Despite a change of name the company struggled to stay afloat in the lean years of the 1920s. Attempts to build civil airliners were commercially unsuccessful but included the four-engined Bristol Pullman developed from the Braemar bomber which had flown in August 1918 and which was one of the largest aircraft of its time. Interestingly there was a project for a flying boat version to be powered by steam turbines, the machinery being accommodated in the fuselage and the propellers driven by extension shafts. Although this far-fetched idea never progressed beyond the drawing board, it was indicative of the Bristol company's willingness to consider unconventional ideas and apply the latest technology.

With aircraft orders reduced to a trickle, the company was forced to diversify its efforts and so set up an RAF Reserve Flying Training School (FTS) in 1923 based on one of the former AAP hangars. Its chief instructor was Cyril Unwins who had flown as an RFC pilot in France and later became Bristol's chief test pilot, flying all Bristol prototypes up to 1947 when he then became a company director. Among the aircraft used were trainer versions of the ubiquitous Bristol Fighter, most of them powered by the Bristol-produced Jupiter radial engine.

The Bristol Aeroplane Company had reluctantly became involved in aero engine production following pressure from the Air Ministry to take over the failed Cosmos company in 1920. Among the latter's range of products was the excellent nine-cylinder Jupiter radial engine designed by Roy Fedden which was rated at 395hp but was subsequently developed to give up to 530hp. The engine business took over one of the AAP hangars on the north-east corner of the airfield and over the following decades was expanded to take over all three hangars as well as new construction on both sides of the Gloucester Road. Initially, however, the board was unhappy at being saddled with the engine business and resolved to close it down at the end of 1921. In the meantime Fedden succeeded in having an engine displayed at the 1921 Paris Salon where it attracted considerable interest and subsequent efforts were eventually rewarded with substantial Air Ministry contracts in 1923. The Jupiter remained in production for ten years with no fewer than 17 foreign licencees being approved. A total of 7,100 engines were built, powering the amazing total of 262 different types of aircraft. The success of this engine was a major element in sustaining the parent Bristol Aeroplane Company through the lean years of the 1920s and early 1930s.

Although efforts to produce civil transport aircraft were generally unsuccessful, the company along with other British manufacturers produced a series of fighter prototypes in response to various Air Ministry specifications. Eventually Bristol went ahead with the construction of a private venture single-seat fighter powered by a 440hp Bristol Mercury VII. First flown in May 1927 it was eventually ordered into production as the Bristol Bulldog II and deliveries to the RAF commenced in May 1929. In total 360 Bulldog II/IIAs were produced, several going for export, while there were also 59 two-seat trainer versions and small numbers of the Mercury-powered Bulldog III/IV.

With the company now re-established as a major supplier of military aircraft, it produced a series of prototype monoplane fighters and obtained a modest production order for the Type 130 Bombay twin-engined bomber transport, although these were actually produced from 1938 by Short Brothers and Harland at their Belfast factory. The reason for this arrangement was that by then the Filton factory was fully occupied with orders for the Bristol Blenheim light bomber powered by two 840hp Bristol Mercury engines. This famous aircraft was ordered by the Air Ministry after the amazing performance demonstrated by the Bristol Type 142 ordered as a private venture by the newspaper magnate Lord Rothmere. First flown in 1935 it demonstrated a maximum speed 50mph faster than the contemporary Gloster Gladiator biplane fighter which had not even entered service with the RAF at that time. Named "Britain First", the aircraft was presented by Lord Rothmere to the Air Ministry who used it for a succession of tests and trials.

Even before the Type 142 had flown, Bristol's Frank Barnwell had drawn up plans for a bomber version and this was ordered into production in September 1935. Before the prototype had flown in June 1936 export orders had been received from Finland, Lithuania, Turkey and Yugoslavia – these illustrating both the outstanding potential of the aircraft and the effect of the gathering war clouds over Europe. By the outbreak of war in August 1939, Filton was not only producing Blenheims but also the Beaufort torpedo bomber powered by two 1,160hp Bristol Taurus radials and its fighter derivative, the Bristol Beaufighter powered by two 1,400hp Bristol Hercules engines. Based on Filton, the industrial complex required to produced these airframes and engines in quantity was the largest of its kind in the world at that time.

During the inter-war years the military presence at Filton had also increased. Mention has already been made of the Reserve FTS and in 1929 the Air Ministry set up Special Reserve and Auxiliary flying units and one of these, No. 501 (City of Bristol) Squadron, was based at Filton. As a bomber squadron it was initially equipped with World War I-era DH-9As but these were quickly replaced by Westland Wapitis which were powered by the ubiquitous Jupiter engine. In 1936 it re-equipped with

Hawker Hinds and was retitled No. 501 (County of Gloucester) Squadron Royal Auxiliary Air Force. In 1939 it reformed as a fighter squadron with Hurricanes but moved to France in 1940.

The Filton complex was obviously a tempting target for the Luftwaffe and with bases in France was easily in range of German bombers. Nevertheless it was not until 25 September 1940 that a major attack was mounted, when He111s of KG55 dropped hundreds of bombs fell on the airfield and factories. Despite the provision of numerous air raid shelters around 90 people were killed and many others injured. On the other hand relatively little serious damage was done to the production facilities, which were quickly back in action. The airfield defences were improved and a fighter squadron (504) was moved in. These were sufficient to keep serious raids at bay, although a night raid in

Right: Although designed as a bomber, the performance of the Blenheim was such that it was also used as a night fighter and was the first to be equipped with airborne interception radar.

April 1942 managed to destroy the wind tunnel building. By the end of 1941 all operational squadrons had moved out of Filton, although at the same time two tarmac runways were laid down to cater for the intensive test flying of a new larger and heavier aircraft in all weathers. Filton then became a centre for aircraft preparation and ferrying. No. 2 Aircraft Preparation Unit was responsible for processing aircraft to be ferried to RAF units abroad while in 1943 the US Army Air Force (USAAF) set up No. XI Base Aircraft Assembly Depot on the north-west side of the airfield. The latter's function was to take aircraft brought by sea to nearby Avonmouth docks and prepare them for issue to UK-based USAAF units.

With the end of the war in sight the government set up a committee under the chairmanship of Lord Brabazon of Tara in 1943 to draw up specifications for

Left: A total of 5,564 Beaufighters were produced in the UK as well as another 364 in Australia. The final production version was the TF.X –a radar-equipped strike aircraft armed with bombs, rockets or a torpedo.

a new range of civil aircraft in the postwar era. The flagship project was a huge 100-seat airliner designed for the prestige North Atlantic route and capable of flying London–New York non-stop at a cruising speed of 300mph. Although having little experience of building very large aircraft, in a surprise move the Bristol company was awarded the contract for the Brabazon (named after the committee chairman) as more obvious candidates such as Avro and Handley Page were fully committed to the production of urgently needed Lancaster and Halifax bombers. In its final form the Brabazon weighed in at 130 tons fully loaded and with a span of 230ft and length 177ft it was the largest airliner in the world until the advent of the Boeing 747 in 1969. The prototype was powered by eight 2,500hp Bristol Centaurus engines coupled to four contra rotating propellers but the projected Brabazon II would have been powered by four 7,000hp Proteus turboprops.

The Brabazon project had an enormous impact on the airfield at Filton. In order to accommodate the massive aircraft, the main east-west runway was widened to 300ft and almost doubled in length by a major westward extension. This controversially required the demolishing of Charlton village. On the south side of the runway, from which it was separated by a railway line, the massive new Aircraft Assembly Hall (AAH) was erected: at the time of its completion in 1948 it was the largest

Below right: In order to extend Filton's runway in preparation for the Brabazon the village Charlton had to be demolished and its residents rehoused, a considerable upheaval for all concerned.

Below: Earthmoving equipment at work on the runway extension which was completed in 1948.

building of its type in the world. A three-bay structure, access was on its south side through folding doors spanning the full 1,052ft width. An aircraft parking apron and a taxiway which incorporated a railway level crossing allowed access to the airfield and runway.

The Brabazon first flew on 4 September 1949. Despite its great size, it was straightforward to handle and the lengthened runway proved more than adequate. However, technical problems delayed the completion of the Proteus-powered Brabazon II which never flew and financial and political considerations eventually led to the abandonment of the project, the two airframes being broken up in 1953. Fortunately Bristol

The Brabazon prototype prepares to take off on its maiden flight, 4 September 1949.

G-AGPW

had many other projects in hand and was busy throughout early postwar years. A notable success was the Bristol Type 170 Freighter and its derivatives, of which 214 were produced between 1945 and 1948. Another promising design, which had its origins in the Brabazon Committee specifications, was the turboprop Britannia long-range airliner. Powered by four Proteus turboprops, the design drew heavily on experience gained with the Brabazon and the prototype Britannia flew for the first time on 16 August 1952. Unfortunately the test programme was set back when the second prototype had to make a forced landing on the mud banks of the Severn estuary following an engine fire. Additionally, after deliveries had commenced to BOAC, problems were experienced with engine flame outs due to icing. Consequently it was not until 1957 that revenue-earning flights commenced, but the long-range 300 series proved popular with some foreign airlines, notably El Al which used the aircraft to fly non-stop from Tel Aviv to New York. In addition, 20 Britannias were ordered for use by RAF Transport Command for long-distance trooping flights. Despite these orders, only 82 Britannias were produced and the last was delivered in 1959. Technically, in terms of performance, range, economy of operation and passenger comfort, the Britannia was an excellent aircraft. However, by the time the aircraft was ready for service the airlines were looking towards the new generation of jets exemplified by the Boeing 707 and DC-8.

The Britannia were built in the AAH which also found several other practical uses. Between 1948 and 1954 the western bay was allocated to BOAC who used it as a maintenance base for American-built Constellations and Stratocruisers. In the early 1950s over 80 Boeing B-29 Superfortress bombers were modified at Filton for the RAF as the Washington B.1. With the rundown of Britannia production, the AAH was used for overhaul and maintenance of Canberras and V-bombers.

Filton's resident RAuxAF Squadron 501 returned in May 1946 equipped with Spitfires and subsequently Vampire jet fighters. Along with the other auxiliary squadrons it was stood down and disbanded in 1957, although the triple-bay hangar adjacent to Hayes Lane which it occupied is still referred to as "501 Hangar". Military flying training also resumed in 1947 with the formation of No. 12 Reserve Flying School and, in

Below: The figures in the foreground give scale to the size of the Brabazon and the enormous Aircraft Assembly Hall built to house the production line.

1950, the Bristol University Air Squadron. As far as the airfield was concerned, the next major development was the construction in 1958 of an Operational Readiness Platform for four V-bombers on the north side of the airfield. Although no V-bomber squadrons were based at Filton, detachments would standby on the dispersals during exercises or times of tension. With the demise of the V-bomber force in the 1970s the ORP provided excellent parking facilities for civil aircraft.

The 1960s were a time of great change for Filton and the Bristol Aeroplane Company. The aero engine division was merged with Armstrong Siddeley in 1950 to form Bristol Siddeley, while the aeroplane company was merged with English Electric and Vickers in 1960 to become the British Aircraft Corporation (BAC). These consolidations reflected the run down in British aircraft production

Right: Concorde 002, the British prototype, is towed out at Filton in preparation for its first flight which took place on 9 April 1969

with insufficient orders to maintain the previously independent companies. The emphasis also changed, partly for political reasons, to international co-operation and this led to a joint Anglo-French design for a supersonic airliner which became the Concorde. Although a French design existed in the form of the Sud Aviation Super Caravelle, the final design was closely based on the Bristol Type 223 project while the Olympus engine was a Bristol Siddeley design originally intended for the cancelled TSR2 bomber. It can be seen that the technical expertise to develop Concorde solely as a British aircraft existed at Filton but the cost of the project and political expediency resulted in the joint project with assembly lines at Filton (in the AAH) and Toulouse. In fact it was the French prototype (001) which flew first on 2 March 1969, the British prototype (002) following a few weeks later on 9 April. Despite a modest extension to the runway at Filton, the prototype was flown to nearby Fairfield where all flight testing was subsequently conducted until 1976. It was an unqualified technical success but many factors resulted in production

being limited to a total of 20 airframes including prototypes and pre-production aircraft and half of these were built at Filton. In fact Concorde was the last complete airframe to be constructed at Filton and the last example was rolled out in 1979.

Already BAC had ceased to exist having been merged in 1977 with the rival Hawker Siddeley Group to form British Aerospace (BAe). The new company became a formal partner in the European Airbus consortium in 1979 and lobbied hard for the production of the new A320 twinjet airliners to be established at Filton, which would have been an ideal location. However this was not to be and BAe had be content with wing production (which was later transferred to Chester). In fact, as related in the next chapter, Airbus was to become the key industrial player at Filton. In the meantime the AAH continued to earn its keep in the 1970s and 1980s as BAe gained contracts to convert surplus VC-10s and Super VC-10s to tanker/transports for the RAF, with further contracts in the 1990s. Between 1978 and 1992 USAF F-111s based in Britain were overhauled at Filton in the AAH and an engine-run test facility was built on the north side of the airfield in the area known as "Palm Beach". Subsequently BAe Aviation Services carried out maintenance work on Airbus aircraft and embarked on a programme to convert A300s to freighter configuration. This resulted in the sight of several aircraft parked on the disused cross runway awaiting conversion. In 1999 BAe took over Marconi Electronic Systems and rebranded as BAE Systems, signalling a move away from aviation to broader defence-related projects such as radars, ordnance and naval systems. These moves were reflected at Filton where Aviation Services was closed down in 2002 although new tenants for the AAH included Air Livery and MK Cargo Airlines (see Chapter 4). Already the engine side of the business had disappeared. As part of the consolidation of the British aircraft industry Bristol Siddeley was sold to Rolls-Royce in 1966. They continued to use the airfield test site until 1995 for projects such as the Olympus for the Concorde and the revolutionary vectored-thrust Pegasus engine used by the STVOL Harrier, both

of these world-beating powerplants being original Bristol designs. Subsequently the whole flight test complex and the original Belfast truss hangars were demolished to make way for a Royal Mail sorting office. It is one of the great ironies of Filton that mail from this office was then carried across Bristol by road for loading into aircraft at Lulsgate, now Bristol International Airport.

With the run down of aircraft production, there was an attempt in 1993 to develop regional airline services from Filton but this proposal met fierce local opposition and was dropped. The year before the University Air Squadron had moved out and these events signalled the start of a long decline which was not helped when Air Livery relocated to Manchester in 2009 and MK Airlines closed down in 2010. Since then the main airfield activity has been the operation of corporate shuttles in support of the Airbus operation of which BAE Systems had sold its shareholding in 2006. In April 2011 BAE Systems decided on purely commercial grounds that the airfield was no longer viable and announced that it would close at the end of the following

year, an event which duly came to pass on 21 December 2012.

Thus the curtain was drawn on 102 years of aviation activity during which Filton became a world-beating centre of aeronautical engineering and the scene of many major technological advances before falling into decline. To many people the airfield is much more than a strip of land. It is a place where whole generations of families have worked and contributed to great endeavours. To a great extent Filton is a microcosm of Britain today, a nation with a great past which has sold off the crown jewels and no longer appears to have the capacity to provide inspiration and leadership to the rest of world.

Left: An aerial view of the Aircraft Assembly Hall in 1997 with a pair of Airbus A300s ready for conversion to freighters. Note the railway level crossing at top right where the taxiway to the runway crosses the line.

Homecoming! One of the last airworthy Concordes lands at Filton on 26 November 2003 where it was subsequently put on display. Currently it is not open to the public but will eventually form the centrepiece of a new aviation heritage site due to open in 2016.
P.R.March

2. AIRBUS AT FILTON

In its closing decade, activity at Filton devolved almost entirely around the activities of the European Airbus consortium. This international organisation was born in the 1960s following a conference in 1967 between representatives of the British, French and German governments who resolved to set up an organisation provide a European aerospace capability to contest the American supremacy in the design and production of commercial jet aircraft. Just two years later, at the 1969 Paris Air Show, the Airbus A300 was officially launched. It was a 250-seater wide-bodied twinjet whose design was very similar to

Hawker Siddeley's HBN100 designed at Hatfield in conjunction with the French companies Breguet and Nord. Initially the British government had financially backed Hawker Siddeley's involvement in Airbus but in April 1969 this support was withdrawn leaving the company out on a limb. However, as the designers of the wing they were in a strong position and eventually secured a 20% share in Airbus and retained overall design authority for the wing. Effectively Hawker Siddeley was a subcontractor to Airbus, but when the company eventually became part of British Aerospace, the new corporation negotiated at government level to rejoin Airbus as a full partner (with a 20% shareholding) in 1978. Britain's role was to provide a centre of excellence for wing design and construction and initially much of this was based on Filton. Over the years BAe (and BAE Systems) gradually moved wing assembly to Broughton, Chester, leaving Filton responsible for various components and wind-tunnel testing, as well fuel system and landing gear development. In 2001 the international Airbus consortium was transformed into a new fully commercial

Left: In the latter years visits by Airbus company aircraft were a rare event. This photo shows one of the few occasions when the A340-600 came to Filton. This long range variant was powered by four Rolls-Royce Trent engines.

Below: A close-up view of the Sharklets fitted to the Airbus A320.

FILTON: END OF AN ERA

Below: The A380 is towed into position on the main runway ready for departure. Despite the immense size of the aircraft it is dwarfed by the scale of the double-width runway and wide turning circle at Filton, these having been laid down originally for the Brabazon.

Below Right: An A380 about to touch down at Filton in February 2008. On this occasion the aircraft was involved in trials with new biofuels on which one of the engines was modified to run.

company, Airbus SAS, which resulted in BAE Systems handing over their factories at Filton and Chester to the new concern.

From 2005 onwards work began at Filton on the production of complete wing sets for the new Airbus A400M turboprop military transport, these being flown to the final assembly plant at Seville by specially adapted Beluga transports. In a further upheaval Airbus sold its wing structure and component elements, including A400M wing production, at Filton to GKN Aerospace in 2008 with the latter now acting as major subcontractor to Airbus, employing some 1,500 staff at Filton. Looking to the future a new dedicated composite manufacturing facility will use the latest in automated composite manufacturing technologies to produce wing trailing edge and wing spar and assemblies for the new Airbus A350XWB which is expected to make its first flight towards the end of 2013.

Despite the massive investment in the factory facilities, Airbus actually made very little direct use of the airfield at Filton, the most obvious activity in recent years being the occasional Beluga flight to collect completed A400M wing sets. These were loaded onto the aircraft via a specially constructed dock on the

The wings for the Airbus A400M military transport are constructed at Filton and facilities including this loading dock were put in place so that the wing sets in specially designed jigs could be pushed into the waiting A300-600ST Beluga.

The first visit to Filton by an Airbus A380 occurred on 18 May 2006 when this aircraft made a low approach without landing before continuing on to London's Heathrow airport. In the background the airfield is surrounded by crowds anxious to get a glimpse of the huge airliner

north side of the airfield. With the closure of Filton these will now have to be moved by road and sea. Other aircraft have visited for fuel trials using the fuel test rig established on the industrial site near the AAH. Here aircraft can be loaded with special fuels, or standard fuels pre-heated to simulate tropical service conditions, for various test flights. However such activities were relatively rare and many Airbus operations into Filton were simply showing the flag – letting their workforce actually see the aircraft in whose design and construction they were involved.

Below: An unusual visitor in January 2012 was this A320 fitted with experimental upswept wingtips known as "sharklets" in Airbus parlance. Such extensions were already common on the rival Boeing 737 and help to increase fuel efficiency by reducing aerodynamic drag.

Right: With the wing sets safely stowed, a Beluga freighter lifts off from Filton's runway at the start of the two-hour flight to Seville where the A400M final assembly line is located.

*Right: A contrast of old and new, large and small.
A restored two-seater Spitfire Mk.IX taxies past a
parked A380 in September 2010.*

*Above: The Airbus A400M military transport has
suffered from an extended development period but
as of 2012 it is full-scale production with 25 on order
for the RAF. One of the prototypes is shown landing
at Filton for fuel trials in June 2012.*

3. THE CORPORATE SHUTTLES

Airbus is a truly international concern with production and design facilities in France, Germany, Britain and Spain. To go about its daily business it needs to transfer hundreds of staff each day between its various centres. Contrary to popular perception these are not just senior executives but ordinary staff such as engineers, draughtsmen, computer technicians and administration workers.

As far as Filton was concerned the main connection was to the Airbus production centre at Toulouse, which was served by daily flights. There was also a connection with the wing production centre at Broughton. In addition BAe and BAE Systems needed to connect Filton with various other UK sites including Barrow-in-Furness, Warton and Glasgow. Initially most of these services were operated by company-owned and operated aircraft, but gradually most

were transferred to commercial airline operators under contracts which were regularly reviewed and sometimes reallocated. The result over the years has been a variety of aircraft in different liveries, many of which are shown in the accompanying photographs.

On busy days several hundred passengers would be handled – always done to airline standards. The increasing terrorism threat to air travel meant that the airport had to provide full security and screening facilities and comply with Department of Transport rules and procedures. The Flight Operations building at the airport entrance, therefore, served as a passenger terminal with check-in and baggage-handling facilities, and holding lounges for departing passengers who would be transported to waiting aircraft by bus.

With the closure of Filton shuttle

flights to Broughton and Toulouse will continue, but these will fly from Bristol International Airport at Lulsgate, necessitating a commute across Bristol for most passengers. They may well ponder as to whether any financial savings which may have accrued from the closure of Filton and the transfer of flights is worth the additional stress of the extra surface journeys.

Barrow-in-Furness is where BAE Systems build submarines and regular daily flights are made by Beech King Air turboprop executive aircraft using the callsign "Vickers", a reference to the original founders and owners of the shipyard at Barrow. Their passengers are generally headed to the BAE/MBDA site at Filton or the the MoD complex at nearby Abbey Wood. These flights will now operate into Gloucester Airport with the passengers being brought onwards by road.

Below: While the Privat Air A319 flew out to Toulouse early in the morning and returned in the evening, the reverse service originating in Toulouse was flown by one or two Aerospatiale SN601 Corvettes as shown here on the ramp at Filton in March 2007

For several years until 2008 the Filton
Toulouse shuttle was operated by Privat Air,
a Swiss charter airline specialising in this
type of work. Appropriately the aircraft used
was an Airbus A319 which is shown taxiing
to the runway for departure.

Above: At one time a daily service to the Airbus plant at Bremen was operated by the German airline OLT (Ostfriesiche Lufttransport GmbH) using Saab 2000 turboprops. The operation was transferred to Bristol International airport in 2006 in order to attract additional business passengers.

Right: Shuttle flights between Filton and Broughton (Chester) and Warton (Preston) were flown by Eastern Airlines using British Aerospace Jetstream 41s.

FILTON: END OF AN ERA

Below: In the summer of 2009 a major reorganisation resulted in flights between Broughton, Filton and Toulouse being operated by British Midland Regional using Embraer 145 50-seater jets. By that time the network of BAE Systems flights to Warton and Scotland had already ceased to operate.

Right: British Midland and its regional subsidiary were members of the Star Alliance group and some of the Embraers were finished in a livery displaying the logos of the member airlines.

3. The Corporate Shuttles

Above Left: BAE Systems also operated flights to and from Glasgow in respect of the shipbuilding activities on the Clyde, and further Naval Systems-related flights were also flown for short period between Scotland, Filton and Plymouth. These were all operated by Highland Airways using Jetstream 31s.

Below Left: An Eastern Airlines Jetstream 41 taxying at Filton showing the striking new livery adopted in 2007.

Below: Occasionally OLT would substitute a smaller Saab 340 on the Bremen route. This one displays the revised livery adopted in 2006.

An Embraer 145 waits in the evening sunshine at the holding point while a Beech King Air lands after a flight from the BAE Naval Systems base at Barrow on Furness.

Above: In 2008 the Toulouse shuttle service was taken over WDL Aviation, a German airline based in Cologne. The aircraft used was a British Aerospace 146 Series 200 shown here on the runway at Filton passing the AAH.

4. THE AIRPORT AT WORK

Running an airport to support commercial and other flights is a complex affair. The design, layout and facilities provided must comply with strict Civil Aviation Authority requirements before an airfield licence is issued. In addition there are stringent regulations covering the security of aircraft, crews and passengers. Adherence to all of these requirements and regulations is regularly checked by inspectors from the CAA and the Department of Transport.

As with most airports the staff work in various departments, each with its own responsibilities. The operational control and safety of aircraft taking off and landing at the airfield was ensured by the air traffic control team supported by air traffic engineers who looked after the complex radio, radar and electronic navigation aids with which Filton was well equipped. The airport had its own

fire station, located adjacent to the east end of the runway, while for the airfield itself there was an operations department responsible for the provision and maintenance of various facilities and fittings including the all-important runway and approach lighting. Ground handling staff were responsible for looking after aircraft and their passengers once they had landed and the encompassed a wide range of tasks including marshalling, baggage handling, operating ground-support equipment and providing transport around the airfield for passengers and crews. In addition they operated various specialist equipment such as aircraft de-icers, runway sweepers and, when required, snow-clearance equipment.

It is an unfortunate fact of life today that air travel is subject to external threats: a team of security staff worked under contract to provide screening of passengers and their baggage, set up protected areas around aircraft on the ground and carried out regular patrols around the airfield and its installations. The Rescue and Firefighting Service (RFFS) at Filton, in addition to providing fire and rescue services to cover actual or potential aircraft incidents, had other ancillary duties at Filton including carrying out regular patrols of the runway and its environs to ensure that it was kept clear of bird concentrations.

The work of some of the individuals who together formed the very efficient Filton Airport team is shown in this short chapter.

Right: The safety of aircraft taking off and landing at Filton was the responsibility of Air Traffic Control (ATC). The control tower building dated from World War II but was upgraded in the 1970s. In the foreground are wild flowers growing on the site of the disused signal square.

Overleaf: An ATC assistant enters data into the Flight Data Management System while in the background a Beluga freighter prepares for departure.

Above: Snow-clearance duties were shared between fire service and ground-handling staff. Here a Sicard brush is in the final stages of clearing the runway surface. This equipment is effective in clearing snow, which is then blown to the side of the runway although the resulting snowbanks then need clearing by other specialised equipment.

Below: As well as the runway, it was necessary to clear taxiways and parking aprons so that the airfield could remain open. Inevitably, having once cleared the airfield another fall of snow would mean that the whole task would have to be repeated!

Heavy snowfall approaching Christmas 2009 seriously affected operations at the airport even if it did present a seasonal image.

Left: The sale of surplus land on the north side of the airfield released funds for updating airfield facilities. To replace the V-bomber ORP this new parking apron was completed in 2009, although unfortunately its use was subsequently restricted due to problems with the concrete surface.

Right: The new S511 radar operated on a shorter wavelength (10cm instead of 50cm) and consequently required a smaller and lighter aerial than the S264 visible in the background.

Left: A close-up of the digital radar display at Filton. The horizontal blue lines mark the final approach tracks to the runways, the orange lines mark airspace associated with Bristol International Airport, while the white alpha-numeric data blocks show information on individual aircraft.

Below: All airports are required to maintain a Rescue and Fire Fighting Service (RFFS) to be available in case of an accident or an emergency. Thankfully such events are very rare, but Filton's RFFS maintained a high standard through constant training and simulated emergency exercises.

Above: Filton was unique amongst British airfields in that a railway line ran through it. Here a VC-10 in primer paint waits at the crossing while an EWS freight train passes. Hidden in the cutting just off to the left of this image are long platforms which would have made an ideal station if Filton had ever developed as a regional airport.

Right: In the 1960s a Marconi S264H long-range radar was installed to support the extensive test-flying activity of the time. It was finally replaced by a more modern S511 in 2009. Here airport staff, including the ATC engineers and the airport manager, pose in front of the massive 264 aerial just before it was dismantled and removed.

5. THE BIG BOYS

Any flight into Filton by the Airbus A380, currently the world's largest airliner, was obviously an event of great interest and attracted crowds of sightseers. However the airport was no stranger to large aircraft with a history going back to the Bristol Braemar in 1918 and the Brabazon in 1949, itself the largest airliner in the world at that time. In recent years the airport was routinely host to the Boeing 747 which first flew in 1969 and was in turn the world's largest airliner until the advent of the Airbus A380 in 2005.

The large AAH hangar at Filton was ideally suited to accommodating such large aircraft and so it was not surprising that MK Airlines should set up their engineering and maintenance base at the airport in 2003. MK was a specialist cargo airline operating mainly between Europe and Africa with a fleet of Boeing 747 and McDonnell Douglas

DC-8 freighters although it did not actually operate any commercial flights from Filton, only positioning aircraft for maintenance. Although a British company, its headquarters was nominally in Ghana where all the aircraft were registered. Following a fatal accident which destroyed one of its 747s taking off from Halifax, Canada in 2004 the airline transferred all aircraft to the British register to comply with European airworthiness requirements and adopted the name British Global although the aircraft still retained the MK titles. The airline had financial problems, going into administration and ceasing operations in June 2008. Subsequently it restarted flights but was finally closed down in April 2010. The airline had the distinction of being one of the last operators of the DC-8 in Europe and so Filton was host to what was becoming a very rare aircraft in European skies. MK also carried out third-party engineering work which resulted in the occasional movement by 747s flown by other airlines. MK also took on a couple of executive aircraft including a private 727 which was a static feature at the airfield for many years.

Another source of large jet movements was Air Livery which leased the east bay of the AAH in 2003. This company specialised in the painting of aircraft, a complex technical task, and their services were much in demand, particularly by leasing companies who would have aircraft flown in at the end of a lease to be repainted in the livery

of a new customer airline. Although Air Livery also had premises at Southend, this could not accommodate the larger aircraft and so not only 747s but other large jet airliners such as the Boeing 767 and 777 and Airbus A330 and A340 were regular visitors. Air Livery moved to Manchester in 2009 and the loss of this company and MK Airlines collapse undoubtedly had a serious detrimental affect on the financial viability of the airfield.

Below: MK Airlines were a major operator at Filton from 2003 until they ceased operating in 2010. Shown here is one of the Boeing 747 fleet, registration G-MKLA.

The Airbus A340 was a comparatively rare visitor to Filton. This British-registered A340-300 (G-VBUS) was owned by Virgin Atlantic but repainted at Filton on 2007 for lease to Air Comet, a short-lived Spanish charter airline.

Above: Another Gulf state visitor in 2007 was this Emirates Airbus A330-200. The airline's aircraft were regular visitors to Filton for attention from Air Livery.

Right: A dramatic shot of a Boeing 747-422 (A6-MMM) lifting off from runway 09 at Filton. This aircraft is a VIP transport operated by the Dubai government's Air Wing.

One of the last aircraft to pass through the Air Livery paint shed before the company relocated to Manchester was this Boeing 767-306ER (HA-LHC) landing on 23 June 2009. Although wearing the distinctive colours of Russian operator S7 Airlines, it is actually registered to Malev, the Hungarian state airline.

Above: MK were one of the last operators of the once numerous DC-8. This example parked at Filton in 2005 is a DC-8-55F (9G-MKF) powered by Pratt & Whitney JT3D turbofans, which offered much-improved fuel efficiency compared with the JT3A/C used on earlier models.

Below: An MK Airlines Boeing 747-2R7F in bare metal finish lands at Filton in September 2007. At that time this aircraft was still wearing its Ghanaian registration 9G-MKL while the MK fleet included no fewer than eight 747s

Another 747 with a chequered history. This 747-219B was delivered to Air New Zealand in 1982 and subsequently served with Malaysia Airlines, Airtours and Virgin before being leased to Transaero in 2005.

5. THE BIG BOYS

Left: A Boeing 777-35RER (VT-JED) of the Indian airline Jet Airways touches down on Runway 27 on 16 December 2008. Boeing 777s from Emirates were also to be seen at Filton on occasions.

Below: A Douglas DC-8-63 (9G-FAB) landing at Filton in August 2006. The stretched version of the DC-8 was known as the Super 60 and this particular aircraft belonged to Johnsons Air, another Ghana-based operator.

Left: This DC-8-63 (9G-MKO) is shown at Filton in June 2005 wearing MK logos but was transferred to Johnsons Air shortly afterwards.

Below Left: This Boeing 747-267B parked at Filton in 2005 had a chequered history. Delivered to Cathay Pacific in 1992, it was later sold to Virgin Atlantic and in 2003 passed to European Air Charter who prepared it for lease to the Argentine airline Southern Winds whose livery it wears. European ceased trading in 2004 and the aircraft sat at Filton for a couple of years before being bought by the Russian Transaero in 2006.

6. THE WORLD'S AIRLINERS

Mention has already be made of Air Livery and the fact that it brought several large aircraft to Filton. It worked on all sizes of commercial airliner and consequently provided many interesting aircraft over the years, some of which were very rare visitors to the UK and would not normally be seen at regular commercial airports.

Routine airline flights were, of course, the various Airbus and BAE shuttles but occasionally if the normal airline had a problem with aircraft servicability they would sometimes charter an aircraft from another operator at short notice. In addition Airbus would sometimes organise events at Filton with staff flown in from France, Germany and other European countries on specially charted flights from some interesting airlines.

Bristol's main commercial airport at Lulsgate is situated on a ridge several hundred feet above sea level and has serious issues with poor weather, particularly when a damp southwest wind causes hill fog or low lying stratus cloud to form over the airfield. In such conditions Filton, being at a lower altitude would have a higher cloud base making it suitable as a diversion airfield for aircraft unable to land at Lulsgate. In recent years Bristol International Airport has been equipped with a Category III Instrument Landing System (ILS) which permits modern airliners to land in conditions of very low visibility. Not all aircraft are so equipped and occasionally such aircraft would divert to Filton for landing. Unfortunately Filton had only limited passenger-handling facilities so was unable to accept the larger aircraft such as a Boeing 737 except in an emergency situation but nevertheless smaller business aircraft and commuter

Aircraft operated or leased by the airlines of states previously part of the Soviet Union were a common sight at Filton as they were repainted in their new liveries. This Airbus A320-233 looks resplendent in the colours of Air Moldova is shown taking off from Runway 27 in April 2009

Previously flown by charter airline My Travel and still wearing the British registration G-SSAS, this Airbus A320-231 is finished in the colours of the Ukraine airline Donbassaero as it prepares to depart from Filton in April 2006.

airliners such as the Dornier Do.228 were sometimes to be seen.

During 2006 Bristol International's runway was being resurfaced, the work being done in stages at night to avoid disruption to scheduled passenger services. Consequently for several months the mail flights which operated at night were transferred to Filton, a move which delighted the Royal Mail officials who now only needed to move the mail a few yards from the sorting office to the aircraft rather than driving across Bristol each night. Interestingly these nightly movements by jet and turboprop aircraft brought no noise complaints from local residents, the fear of such complaints being one of the reasons for setting up the flights from Bristol International in the first place!

Below: This A320-214 is finished in the colours of the Russian airline Vladivostock Air. Appropriately it has a light dusting of snow at Filton in February 2009.

Below Right: A Boeing 737-8S3 of the Turkish carrier Pegasus Airlines taxies onto the runway for departure from Filton, 2 April 2009. This is one of the new New Generation variants of the best selling 737 and is fitted with upswept winglets for improved fuel efficiency.

An airline colour scheme not normally seen in the UK is that of Sun County Airlines based in Minneapolis-St. Paul in the United States. Previously flown by Easyjet, this Boeing 737-73V has just been rolled out of the Air Livery paint shop in February 2009 prior to delivery across the Atlantic to its new owner.

The Fokker 100 was one of the most successful
European jet airliners, with a total of 283
delivered between 1986 and 1997. It was a
rare visitor to Filton, this example operated by
a French charter airliner arriving on 13 January
2009 carrying visitors to the Airbus factory

An exotic visitor! This Boeing 737-4Z6 belongs to the Thai government and is here flown by a member of the Thai royal family for a training approach and landing at Filton, 11 July 2012.

Above: Another 800 series Boeing 737 landing at Filton in January 2006 – this aircraft belongs to the Cypriot airline Helios which had suffered a fatal accident when one of their aircraft crashed in August 2005 due to crew incapacitation. Subsequently the airline ceased operations a few months after this photo was taken.

Left: Another aircraft far from home is this Boeing 757-256ET in the colours of Air Niugini preparing to depart from Filton on 6 December 2008 for its base at Port Moresby in Papua New Guinea. It was previously operated by Icelandair and still bears the Icelandic registration TF-FIY.

During the summer of 2006 Royal Mail postal flights operated out of Filton while Bristol International's runway was being resurfaced at night. Among the aircraft involved was this Fokker F27 Friendship belonging to the Turkish airline MNG Kargo.

7. MILITARY VISITORS

Although a private airfield in its final decades, Filton had many military connections and indeed was an active RFC airfield in the First World War and an RAF airfield during and after the Second. The last military aircraft permanently based at Filton were the Bulldogs of the Bristol University Air Squadron and its associated Air Experience Flight, which moved out in 1992. Over the years a steady stream of military aircraft has visited the airfield for a variety of reasons, one of which is the proximity of the Ministry of Defence Procurement Executive establishment at nearby

Below: Armed to the teeth, a Panavia Tornado GR.4 taxies at Filton, October 2007. The aircraft carries the markings of No. 41 Squadron based at Marham in Norfolk.

Abbey Wood. This modern complex was opened in 1996 and has been considerably expanded over the years. Currently some 10,000 staff work there and necessary liaison between Abbey Wood and operational units has brought not only communications aircraft such as the Dominie and various helicopters

Below: A Boeing E-3 Sentry taxies onto the runway for a flight back to its base at RAF Waddington in Lincolnshire. It bears the markings of No. 8 Squadron on the forward fuselage but on the other side are the red and blue No. 23 Squadron markings. At the time the two squadrons operated pooled aircraft, hence the two sets of markings, although No. 23 Squadron has since been disbanded.

but also aircraft from operational and training units. Consequently over the years Filton has seen representatives of almost all RAF front-line aircraft types as well as the Tucanos and Hawks from Nos. 1 and 4 Flying Training Schools.

Perhaps the most noticeable military visitors to Filton have been the famous RAF Red Arrows display team. Although they did not actually perform at Filton in recent years, they flew in on several occasions to use the airfield as a base for displays at various West Country locations such as Weston-super-Mare and Torbay. Even so their arrivals and departures were spectacles in themselves, the team maintaining the highest standards of airmanship and teamwork from start up to shut down.

Until 2011 the nearest major military airfield was Lyneham, home to the RAF's fleet of C-130 Hercules transports which subsequently moved to Brize Norton. This latter base is now the UK's main military transport hub operating VC-10s, Tristars, C-17 Globemasters as well as the newly based Hercules (and the recently introduced Voyager tanker based on the Airbus A330). All of these were regular visitors to Filton for training purposes and could be seen flying practice instrument approaches although rarely actually landing. Nevertheless the sight of a huge C-17 on final approach crossing over the A38 must have given many a motorist a surprise.

One of the transport types which did land regularly was the VC-10, often flying into Filton for painting by Air Livery after undergoing a major overhaul at RAF St. Athan near Cardiff. On these occasions the aircraft would arrive in a bare metal primer finish and leave a few days later resplendent in the standard low visibility grey colour scheme. In service for over 40 years, the VC-10 is still one of the most graceful (if noisy) aircraft ever flown, but they will be phased out in the near future as the new Voyager multi-role tanker transports (MRTT) are delivered.

Foreign military aircraft were rare visitors to Filton but the occasional liaison flight would arrive bringing officials visiting Abbey Wood, BAE or Rolls-Royce. The latter would sometimes arrange special events which would bring military visitors to Filton – perhaps one of the most significant was the opening of their new £75 million factory complex on the Filton East site by Princess Anne on 17 October 2008. This was marked a by a dramatic flypast of the Rolls-Royce-owned Spitfire PR.XIX and a Eurofighter.

Below: A flypast by Hawks of the Red Arrows together with a Eurofighter Typhoon at an event in July 2007 sponsored by Rolls-Royce.

Even on the ground the Red Arrows maintain an impeccable formation, as here after landing on the runway at Filton.

FILTON: END OF AN ERA

Below: No. 3 FTS at RAF Cranwell is responsible for multi crew and navigator training at RAF Cranwell and until recently was equipped with BAe Dominies, one of which is shown here at Filton in June 2009. The Dominie entered RAF service in 1965 but has now been replaced in the training role by Beech King Airs.

Above Right: A French Air Force Socoata TMB700 single-engined turboprop communications aircraft at Filton, 28 June 2010.

Below Right: A Shorts Tucano T.I turboprop from No. I FTS based at Linton-on-Ouse in Yorkshire which is responsible for the basic training of RAF pilots. The Tucano is an Anglicized version of the Brazilian Embraer EMB.312 Tucano which is widely used by air forces around the world. In the background of this 2008 photo can be seen one of the surviving World War I Belfast hangars.

Above: A very rare visitor to Filton was this French Air Force C160R Transall tactical transport aircraft pictured in December 2007. Powered by twin Rolls-Royce Tyne turboprops, the Transall was a joint Franco-German project which first flew in 1963, a total of 192 eventually being produced.

Left: A pair of Royal Air Force Eurofighter Typhoons in the markings of No. 3 Squadron at Filton, September 2009.

Above: British Aerospace Harrier GR.9 at Filton in September 2009. At the time the aircraft was part of the Joint Harrier Force (RAF/RN) based at RAF Cottesmore. Following the Strategic Defence Review in 2011 these highly capable aircraft were prematurely withdrawn from service.

Above: This Gulfstream IV executive transport belongs to No. 334 Squadron, Royal Netherlands Air Force, and is seen landing at Filton in November 2007.

BAe Hawks from 4 Flying Training School (FTS) at Valley were frequent visitors to Filton. This example wears the blue and white chequerboard markings of No. 19 (Reserve) Squadron.

8. EXECUTIVE AND GENERAL AVIATION

Although Filton's main activity was the support of Airbus and BAE Systems activities, there have always been a small number of privately owned light aircraft based on the airfield and it has been a popular destination for businessmen or private flyers wishing to visit the Bristol area. As Bristol International has become busy and more commercially orientated, light aircraft would come into Filton to avoid the higher charges. In the last decade there were two flying clubs or flight-training organisations. One was the Bristol Aero Club (BAC) which was set up as a non-profit flying club for BAE and Airbus employees, although in later years it was open to all comers. This operated two Piper Cherokees and was at Filton right up to the last day of operations before moving on to Kemble. The other was Aeros Flight Training, an element of a large commercial flying training

organisation whose headquarters were at Gloucester. The company operated from several other airfields including Filton where at times up to six Cherokees were based.

In the last few years the privately based aircraft began to move away as airport charges were increased, a move compounded when it was decided in 2008 that the airfield would not open at weekends. Following the announcement that the airfield would close permanently at the end of 2012, Aeros moved out in September 2012, having previously scaled down their operation. Paradoxically the impending closure resulted in an increase in light aircraft movements, particularly in the last few weeks, as many pilots took the opportunity to make a landing at Filton before it closed for good. Many of these, or members of their families, had worked at Filton in the past and were making the visit for nostalgic reasons.

Apart from private pilots, Filton was a popular destination for businessmen in their own aircraft or chartered executive jets. The importance of a facility to accommodate such flights to the local community and economy is often overlooked. Landing at Filton, it was easy to arrange a taxi or personal transport to reach an onwards destination and the security procedures were generally much less onerous than at the busier airports. Indeed, it was possible on many occasions for passengers to be driven directly to their waiting aircraft, a much-appreciated facility. As a result Filton was a popular destination for executive jets from around the world, transatlantic

Below: In 1964 the Learjet was amongst the first of the new breed of executive jets and in developed versions has been in continuous production ever since, although the design rights are now owned by the Canadian company Bombardier Aerospace. Shown at Filton in July 2007 is a Learjet 45 operated by Gama Aviation based at Famborough.

departures and arrivals not being unusual. Many of the aircraft belonged to NetJets, a fractional ownership concept which opens up private jet travel to businesses and individuals who might otherwise not consider it. At the top end of the scale were the aircraft owned by major global companies such as Boeing and Rolls-Royce, but almost every type of executive jet has visited Filton at some time or other.

Right: On the lighter-than-air theme is this American Blimp Corporation A60+ airship overflying Filton. Owned by Lightship Europe Ltd. it is acting as a flying advertisment for Goodyear tyres and, as the company name implies, the airship envelope can be lit up at night for added impact.

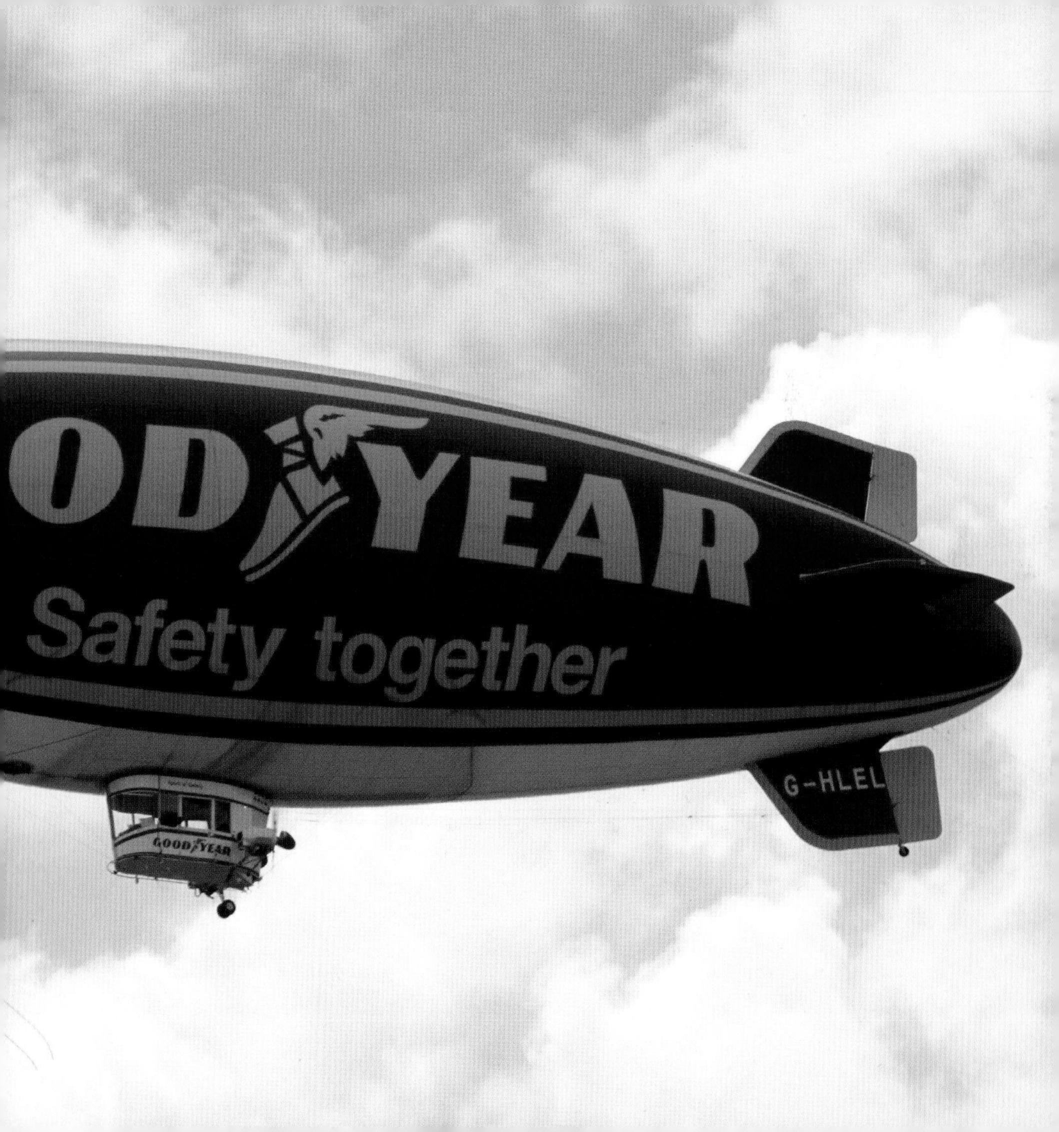
OD YEAR
Safety together
G-HLEL
GOOD YEAR

8. EXECUTIVE AND GENERAL AVIATION

Left: The French company Dassault is the most prolific European manufacturer of business jets. This Swiss registered Dassault Falcon 2000 pictured in September 2006 is operated by Geneva based TAG Aviation. A subsidiary of the TAG Group owns and operates the airfield at Farnborough as an executive jet centre, a role which Filton could well have taken on if the required investments had been available.

Below: NetJets is a major fractional ownership executive jet operator with its European headquarters in Lisbon, Portugal where all its aircraft are registered. This one at Filton in September 2008 is a Hawker 400XP. Originally a Japanese design by Mitsubishi, it was taken up by Beechcraft (Raytheon) and subsequently marketed under the Hawker brand.

The largest executive jets are actually
specialised versions of jet airliners such as
this Boeing Business Jet (BBJ) developed
from the 737. This aircraft is actually owned
by Boeing and flew in their executives to
sign a deal with GKN Aerospace at Filton in
May 2011.

8. EXECUTIVE AND GENERAL AVIATION

Above Left: Visiting Filton in 2008 was an FLS Aerospace Sprint 160, a British design that deserved a better fate. First flown in 1983 as the Trago Mills SAH-1, the design rights passed to various companies including Bournemouth-based FLS who produced three flyable Sprints but ceased trading before series production could begin.

Below Left: Stalwarts of the Filton-based Bristol Aero Club, these two Piper Cherokees were an everyday sight at Filton right up to the last day of operations. The Cherokee first flew in 1960 since when it has become one of the popular light aircraft in the world with well over 40,000 of all variants delivered to date.

Below: This Cherokee Warrior II photographed in 2009 sports the livery of British Overseas Airways Corporation (BOAC) while the side hidden from the camera is painted in British European Airways (BEA) livery as a tribute to the two airlines which merged in 1973 to form British Airways.

Left: Something different! A hot air balloon carrying a waving group of passengers makes a low pass over Filton on a summer's evening in 2005

Above Right: An eye-catching colour scheme adorns this Austrian-registered Diamond DV22 Katana. Like many current light aircraft, the airframe is of composite construction using modern synthetic materials.

Below Right: The world's most prolific business jet is the Cessna Citation of which hundreds have been sold since it first entered service in 1971. A complete redesign of the basic airframe resulted in the CitationJet which flew in 1991 and subsequent improved and enlarged versions became the CJ1, CJ2 and CJ3, examples of the latter two shown parked side by side at Filton in October 2011 (CJ2 nearest).

9. HELICOPTERS

When Filton airport closed at the end of 2012 the only remaining aviation activity was contained in a small enclosed area on the north side of the airfield where emergency service helicopters (Police and Air Ambulance) continue to operate. This is a temporary arrangement as plans exist for a permanent helicopter facility on the south side of the airfield near the existing Flight Operations building. This offers easy access to the A38 main road, although it will only be for use by emergency services and will not be available to other operators

Filton's association with helicopters goes back quite a long time as even during 1944 the Bristol Aeroplane Company had begun working on the design of a practical four-seater helicopter. This eventually became the Type 171 Sycamore, which flew in prototype form on 27 July 1947. After various tests and demonstration flights, the Sycamore was granted the first ever Certificate of Airworthiness issued to a British helicopter on 25 April 1949 and went on to achieve commercial success with a total of 178 being delivered. However after 94 had been built at Filton, production moved to Weston-super-Mare which became the centre of helicopter design and production although flight testing still took place at Filton.

The next Bristol helicopter was the twin-rotor Type 173 originally designed to carry 13 passengers but also suitable for various military roles. Flight trials began in 1952 and in 1956 one of the prototypes was used by the BEA Helicopter Unit for a trial period. A potential order for 50 naval machines was cancelled in favour the Westland-built S-58 (Wessex), but an improved variant powered by two Napier Gazelle turboprops was ordered into production as the Type 192 Belvedere for the RAF, a total of 26 being delivered from 1961 onwards. By that time Bristol Helicopter Department had been taken over by Westland as part of the government-inspired rationalisation of the British aircraft industry. Although Bristol had several interesting projects in hand

Below: The prototype Bristol Type 171 Sycamore helicopter, which first flew on 27 July 1947. This and the second prototype were powered by an American 450hp Pratt & Whitney Wasp Junior engine but subsequent production machines had the British 550hp Alvis Leonides.

including a tilt-wing four-engined vertical take off transport powered by four Rolls-Royce Tyne turboprops, Westland's had a policy of licence production of American Sikorsky designs and the Bristol projects were abandoned.

Once almost solely the preserve of military air arms, helicopters are now widely used for a variety of civil tasks as well as being popular with private and corporate owners. This was readily apparent at Filton where the resident Police Air Support Unit was joined by an Air Ambulance helicopter and, for a short while during the 2012 Olympics, a helicopter was also operated on behalf of Avon and Somerset Fire Service. Helicopters are widely used by public utility companies to inspect and survey electric power lines and gas pipelines, as well as by Network Rail to inspect and monitor railway tracks. All of these concerns would regularly land at Filton for refuelling during their routine patrols. Military helicopters were also much in evidence, often bringing in visitors to the MoD at Abbey Wood as well helicopters from all three services using Filton for training purposes.

Above: A more advanced design was the twin-rotor Type 173. Shown here at Filton in 1956 is the second prototype which is finished in the colours of British European Airways to whom it was loaned for trials, although it wears the military serial XH379. In the background can be seen the north-east hangar complex and the then Bristol Aero Engines works, all of which have since been demolished.

Right: This Agusta A109E helicopter is operated by No. 32 (The Royal) Squadron based at RAF Northolt, and is one of a fleet of three, which were frequent visitors to Filton carrying service or government VIPs and occasionally members of the Royal Family.

A long-time resident at Filton has been the Police Air Support Unit flown on behalf of local forces by the Western Counties Air Operation Unit. In recent years this has flown a Eurocopter EC135 helicopter fitted with various electro-optical devices for surveillance and tracking purposes.

FILTON: END OF AN ERA

Below: In the summer of 2011 the Avon and Somerset Fire Service conducted trials using the chartered Eurocopter EC145 shown here. In response to simulated scenarios a team of six specialist firefighters was airlifted at short notice to various locations to carry out firefighting and rescue exercises.

Below Right: The Great Western Air Ambulance (GWAA) was set up at Filton in 2007 and initially also used a Eurocopter EC135 leased from Bond Helicopters. In common with other UK air ambulance organisations, the GWAA was entirely dependent on charitable donations to cover its running costs.

9. HELICOPTERS

Right: An interesting military visitor was this Agusta Westland AW139 helicopter belonging to the Irish Air Corps which landed at Filton for a refuelling stop on 21 May 2007 after a flight from its base at Baldonnel near Dublin.

Right: A line-up of visiting helicopters at a fly-in to Filton on 26 April 2007. In the foreground is an AS350 Squirrel; then a pair of Robinson R22s and a single R44; and at the far end is an Enstrom 480. Due to their relatively low purchase price and operating costs, the Robinson helicopters are particularly popular with flying training organisations and private owners.

Below: Experience showed that the twin-engined EC135 was too expensive to run on the funding available so the Air Ambulance re-equipped with a smaller single-engined Bölkow Bo.105 which is currently still in service at Filton.

Helicopters are used extensively by public utility companies for surveys and inspections. This Schweizer 330 turboprop light helicopter at Filton in 2008 was on charter to the National Grid and is finished in the black and yellow colour scheme now common amongst public service helicopter operators.

Above: A Westland Aerospatiale Puma HC.1 landing at Filton in April 2006. This troop-carrying helicopter was flown by No. 33 Squadron based at Benson in Oxfordshire and this unit has a particular connection with Filton in that it first formed here in 1916.

Left: Another unusual visitor, in October 2010, was this Sikorsky S-92A belonging to Gulf Helicopters based in Qatar. Powered by two General Electric 2,520shp CT7-8A turboshafts, the S-92A can carry up to 19 passengers.

10. SPITFIRES AND HERITAGE AIRCRAFT

In the years before its closure Filton was one of the few airfields where airworthy Spitfires could be seen regularly. The reason for this was the existence of the Rolls-Royce Heritage Flight, which operated a pristine restored Spitfire PR.XIX, a Griffon-engined unarmed photographic reconnaissance version of this famous fighter. The expertise gathered together under the manager, John Hart, was put to good use in rebuilding and maintaining other privately owned Spitfires. Consequently, particularly on summer weekends, it was not uncommon to see one or two Spitfires departing from Filton en route to a flying display at another airfield. On their return they would inevitably treat the gathered crowd of onlookers to a high-speed low pass before breaking off for a circuit and landing – the sound of a Merlin or Griffon engine at full power

being unforgettable. In 2009 the PR.XIX was moved to East Midlands Airport but other Spitfires were still around right up to the last week that Filton was open. During that last week a Spitfire Mk.IX (RS232), which had been under

Above Right: A colourful visitor to Filton in September 2009 was this de Havilland DH.82A Tiger Moth – the RAF's main primary trainer during World War II. Widely used by civil flying clubs in the postwar era, many still survive today and several are painted in RAF colours to commemorate their military past.

Below Right: Following the de Havilland connection, this pristine de Havilland DH.85 Leopard Moth visited Filton in the summer of 2006. First flown in 1933 and featuring an unusual seating layout with the centrally located pilot ahead of two passengers on a rear bench seat, the Leopard Moth proved very popular and 132 were produced.

Above: Visiting Filton in the summer of 2007 was this P-51D Mustang owned by the Scandinavian Historic Flight based at Oslo in Norway. It is finished in the colour scheme of the 363rd Fighter Squadron, 357th Fighter Group which was part of the US Eighth Air Force based in the United Kingdom.

Below: A nostalgic shot of two Merlin-engined thoroughbreds at Filton in 2007. In the foreground is the Spitfire Mk.VIII and behind is a North American P-51D Mustang powered by a Packard-built Merlin engine

Above: The Hawker Sea Fury FB.11 was the ultimate British piston-engined fighter and saw service with the Royal Navy during the Korean War. The aircraft shown here belonged to the Royal Navy Historic Flight and was participating in an air show arranged for Airbus staff and their families in the summer of 2006.

Below: A natural successor to the famous Tiger Moth, the Chipmunk first flew in 1946 and entered service with the RAF in 1950. Over 60 years later this example still serves with the RAF Battle of Britain Memorial Flight acting as a communications aircraft and providing tailwheel experience to current jet pilots converting onto the flights historic Spitfires and Hurricane.

restoration for some time, made its first test flight before subsequently departing for a new home. John Hart and his team have moved to Kemble where they will continue to be a centre of excellence for Spitfire restoration.

The presence of the Spitfire facility attracted other warbird owners: in particular, a number of Merlin-engined Mustangs came into Filton. They could also be seen at the occasional Airbus family day air shows. Otherwise there were a surprising number and variety of less exotic but still interesting vintage aircraft to be seen on the tarmac at Filton, examples of which are shown in this chapter.

Right: An Auster AOP.9 and a de Havilland Canada DHC-2 Beaver belonging to the Army Air Corps Historic Flight based at Middle Wallop, Hampshire. These two aircraft visited Filton in November 2008 in connection with a local Remembrance Day event which they overflew dropping a shower of poppies.

Below: The Rolls-Royce-owned Supermarine Spitfire PR.XIX lands on Runway 27 at Filton on 22 July 2008. Powered by a 2,050hp Rolls-Royce Griffon engine, the unarmed PR.XIX was one of the fastest versions of the Spitfire with a top speed of 450mph at altitude.

Below: The Royal Navy's Historic Flight also operated a Chipmunk. In fact the Royal Navy operated some of the last military-owned Chipmunks in the UK, using them as part of the Plymouth-based Air Experience Flight attached to the Royal Naval College at Dartmouth until as late as 1993.

Spitfire Mk.VIII MT928 makes a spectacular high-speed run past the control tower in June 2009. This aircraft is painted in the markings of No. 145 Squadron, which was the first to receive this version when it was based in North Africa in 1943. Among its pilots was Neville Duke who became a famous test pilot in the postwar years.

Right: A cockpit view of the Spitfire Mk.VIII, a plaque at top left showing the aircraft's current civil identity, G-BKMI. The high standard of authenticity achieved in the restoration of this aircraft is clearly evident.

Originally built in 1944 as a standard Spitfire MkIX, this aircraft was salvaged from a South African scrapyard and eventually restored by Classic Aeros at Thruxton to represent a Spitfire TR9 two-seat trainer flown by the Royal Netherlands Air Force in the late 1940s. It is shown at Filton a few months after changing hands at auction for the sum of £1,739,500

11. CLOSURE

It had been announced as far back as April 2011 that the airfield at Filton would close at the end of 2012 and the final day of operations was actually Friday, 21 December. In the months leading up to the closure many permanent staff left if they were able to secure alternative employment but nevertheless the airport continued to function normally to the very end with the help of temporary and contract staff. During the last week, on Tuesday 18 December, Airbus flew in an A380 for the last time and this made a local flight carrying various Airbus and Filton staff, flying over Exeter and Bristol before returning to Filton for a last landing. It then departed for Toulouse later in the day. The occasion was favoured with good weather enabling many on the ground to get a good view of the big airliner. Coincidently, it was on this day that Spitfire RS323 made its

first post-reconstruction flight. Several visiting light aircraft added to the party atmosphere, their pilots and passengers being treated to the contrasting iconic sights of the world's largest airliner and one of the most inspiring military aircraft ever built.

The Wednesday and Thursday were relatively quiet days at Filton due to the poor weather but the last day, Friday, dawned clear and bright. Although there was only one scheduled airliner movement, the last BMI Regional flight from Toulouse, there were a large number of private aircraft who flew in that morning, eager to be present on the airport's last day. Just before midday these filed out to the runway under the direction of Air Traffic Control and took off in turn. The last departure fittingly went to a Cessna Citation executive jet piloted by Peter Turner who had a long association with Filton stretching back to 1962 when he made his first flight as an ATC cadet. In later years he flew for both Rolls-Royce and BAC before setting up his own business as an executive jet charter operator. After take off he turned back and made a low pass over the runway, wings dipped in salute.

Climbing away, there was an emotional exchange of messages over the radio with Air Traffic Control and then it was all over.

Truly the end of a great era in British aviation.

Monday, 17 December 2012. Anxious to prepare Spitfire RR232 for its maiden flight before the airfield closes, the restoration team carry out ground runs on the Rolls-Royce Merlin engine.

Well before the date the airfield was scheduled to close, Filton began to receive visitors wishing to make one last call. A poignant example was this Panavia Tornado F.3 making a low pass in July 2012 as it was making the last flight by the interceptor version. Beneath it is the preserved Concorde which will eventually form the centrepiece of the Filton Aviation Heritage Centre.

FILTON: END OF AN ERA

Below: "Cleared for Take Off!" Cessna Citation G-CGEI lines up for the very last departure from Filton's Runway 27 with the Air Traffic Control tower in the background. P.R.March

Above Right: This Piper PA28R Arrow IV was one of many aircraft which flew into Filton on the morning of Friday, 21 December, so that their pilots and passengers could be part of the historic occasion. Fittingly this aircraft was operated by Gloucester-based Aeros Flight Training who themselves had run a Flying School at Filton for many years. P.R.March

Below Right: Tuesday, 18 December. An Airbus A380 arrives to give some Airbus staff a last chance to see and fly in the aircraft they help to produce. After a one-hour local flight in perfect weather conditions, the aircraft is shown landing back at Filton. P.R.March

Above Left: The departure of Spitfire RR232 was a notable event as it was the last of many thousands of aircraft which had their maiden flights at Filton. P.R.March

Below Left: Also on the Tuesday the Spitfire Mk.IX had completed its last checks and is shown taxying out for a departure to a temporary home at nearby RAF Colerne. In the background is one of the British Midland Regional Embraer 145s which will complete the airport's last scheduled service on the following Friday.

Right: Wings dipped in salute, Peter Turner brings the Citation over the runway for a farewell flypast. P.R.March

CENTRAL FIRE STATION

Preparing to depart, the last two aircraft to take off from the runway at Filton. In the foreground is a veteran Cessna 172 owned by aviation journalist and photographer, Peter March, while the Citation executive jet is flown by Peter Turner, a pilot having long associations with Filton. P.R.March

A final view of a now-deserted Filton on its closing day, taken from the Police helicopter. Western Counties Air Operations Unit.

Out on the runway, the airport staff including ATC, engineers, administration and ground handlers gather on the Runway designator numbers for a last farewell. The figure in the centre is the Airport Manager, Alan Haile. Western Counties Air Operations Unit.